I0211023

agriculture of grief
prayers for my father's dementia

New Women's Voices Series, No. 182

poems by

mejdulene bernard shomali

Finishing Line Press
Georgetown, Kentucky

agriculture of grief
prayers for my father's dementia

New Women's Voices Series, No. 182

Copyright © 2024 by mejdulene bernard shomali
ISBN 979-8-88838-676-7 First Edition
All rights reserved under International and Pan-American Copyright Conventions.
No part of this book may be reproduced in any manner whatsoever without written
permission from the publisher, except in the case of brief quotations embodied in
critical articles and reviews.

ACKNOWLEDGMENTS

Versions of "baba's song" and "where does grief live" were previously
published in *Tinderbox* in 2017.
A version of "confirmation" was previously published in *The Adroit Journal*
in 2024.
Versions of "first death" and "ekphrastic" were previously published in *Mizna*
in 2024.

Publisher: Leah Huete de Maines
Editor: Christen Kincaid
Cover Art and Design: Aude Abou Nasr

Order online: www.finishinglinepress.com
also available on amazon.com

Author inquiries and mail orders:
Finishing Line Press
PO Box 1626
Georgetown, Kentucky 40324
USA

Contents

for baba, of course

baptism

dig a well between أسكدنيا & apricot
past topsoil into regolith

let the bedrock be bedrock
settle in & hang pictures at illuviation

picture: a gardener waters his crop
picture: the root & the stalk

picture: sand spots in the humus of his mind
picture: an agriculture of grief

confirmation

a doctor points to gray areas

        see these gray areas

once my father was in full color

        now he has lost some things

he worries the rosary

        wakes screaming with night terrors

a priest sighs حرام a good man

        baba's taken to wearing

the virgin mary around his neck

        a talisman a gold chain

anchored between awake & elsewhere

        grief slouches his shoulders

at a wedding my father is missing

        no one is leading the زفّة

& i can't remember the entire سامر

        just voices cracking

dipped heads & trembling beats

        we find him singing most often

فلسطين تنادیني

        serenading the summer country

its verdant landscape

        burst & blown with color

soaked in fractured sounds

        its rivers rushing him home

we sit in the kitchen

        my mother laments how different he is

while he recites the periodic table

        i tell the story of baba cooking corn

in microwave short minutes

        just four in the husk

just four minutes of clarity

        baba laughs when i tell it

a lesson he remembers

        long enough to remember me

how he taught me these little things

        each moment a balm against forget

eucharist

the first time i see my father's tremors
he passes breadsticks at olive garden

at church he ministers sacrament
places it in upturned palms of believers

soon his script
comes broken & sloppy

soon my mother
begins to feed him

soon his hunger wanes
& he forgets how to swallow

four times a day he spits
medication into her face

his hands clench & nails pierce palm
he cannot control them

his tremors travel from pinky
to torso in trembles & quakes

even sleep cannot quiet
his restless seeking

confession

on its trunk, above human height
a burl grows on a redwood.

knotted & gnarled
a high burl forms in distress

when its parent tree experiences trauma.
my father is old now.

for years i have watched him age.
he has arrived at this place,

old, where his skin is translucent.
i see glass in his eyes.

in the red woods trees filter the sun
illuminate the grove selectively.

in the sun redwoods are truly red.
i hadn't realized.

my father tells me he is dying
inside a mechanic's waiting room.

across from us a family stares away.
pretends not to listen to his harried confession.

pretends not to bury us in their pity.
i stand inside the cavernous belly of a redwood.

rest my head against its damp, cool trunk.
i pray for my father, old in michigan.

      hallowed thine heart
      hallowed this forest of time

        hallowed this girl losing her father
        hallowed all our losses

a burl contains the entire DNA
it needs to reproduce its parent tree.

when a redwood falls, its burl
bends time, becomes its parent's future.

a burl remembers home,
recreates life after it's over.

anointing of the sick

amreeka is a debt paid in bodies & blood
takes everything back plus interest

fuck these doctors & their flaccid solutions
fuck this landscape of settlers & sorrow

in truth i think we own nothing
in truth i think our bodies are borrowed

in truth i pray for god every hour
in truth i already miss my father

god is a crack in the bedrock of myself
god is an apricot still sour

god is a fracture in the lithosphere
god is a fig tree with no flower

i want nothing from this earth or its false gods
i want nothing but my father home

i bury him in the field of myself
i sow his memory & reap my own

penance

forgive me baba
i was scared   i denied
i didn't believe   you would leave us

i couldn't

& now there aren't enough
hail marys in the world
to save him
                my almighty father
slight in his long underwear
his trim mustache   his quiet closed face

for the kingdom & the power & the glory
are buried in our olive groves & citrus fields
      flesh of my father
forsaken in a hostile land
        his mind unraveling in amreeka

forgotten   unmade
god from god   light from light
dear god   dear god

i am sorry with all my heart
i am sorry with all my heart

marriage

my mother took up smoking at sixty-four
her pristine lungs & my father's lewy bodies

two opposing screenings
she was seventeen at marriage

fifty-two years with him
seventy by seven a god she cannot forgive

holy orders

for decades my father worked at a convenience store
sat behind the cash register
stacked two empty pickle buckets as a stool
adorned them with a thin pleather cushion
i imagine my father there
the plastic bucket fractures
grows down & coils into the ground
the cushion becomes dense with foliage & flora
becomes soft & luscious
the stool grows arms & then a back
my father relaxes into it
a throne surging into the sky
its leaves grow overhead as the throne climbs
under its canopy is cool & calm
the convenience store is below
it recedes as the throne grows & grows
soon the store pops like an inflatable bounce house
cans of vegetables & cigarette boxes & 40s become flat things
the more things flatten the higher my father climbs
this continues for a long time before the store door chimes
a customer grabs at the merchandise like a child playing parachute
from the sky my father calls down
there's no one here but the lights & they're going out

viaticum

i am afraid of ghosts. i am afraid of death & its finality. the fear
makes me panic & i can't breathe. when scared i do something
my father taught me. i think of happy things. i used to pray.

i still think of happy things. my first happy thing was birthday
cake. it was the platonic form of birthday cake. the kind my
mother would never make. the kind i wouldn't have liked. as
a kid my goal was sugar consumption in any form. sprinkles
& chocolate chips & buttercream. add sugar to sugar. make
everything sweet & fast.

my happy things cake was two layers of vanilla cake & vanilla
icing. one perfect candle on top. i would sit next to my dad.
during a thunderstorm. after a bad dream. i would think of cake
& pray. our father who art in frosting. hallowed be thy crumb.
thy birthday come. thy wish be done. on earth as it is in heaven.

if heaven were real would i be scared of dying? does heaven
negate the existence of ghosts? do ghosts negate the impact of
death? i still wake up scared. i am scared because my father is
dying. what is a happy thing in proportion to his passing? a
prayer, his birthday, the sweetness of him.

baba's song

when i was two my baba broke his shoulder
so he took a vacation from sixteen hour days on the store floor
& we flew to the بلاد just me & my dad
in a yellow taxicab from the airport in amman
i was so cold in the back seat & baba in front
he covered me with the first thing he could find
a nightgown from our suitcase

at my uncle's house i dance & sing in a red dress
with white dots & my hair is curt around my tiny face
i didn't get fat until i was eight & everyone just loves
this girl who can sing all the folk songs
i am baba's girl through & through
so much that i won't sleep unless he is near me

at twenty-nine i sit at the table with my baba
& we sing "سكّر معمال السكر"
my jam when i was two & we sing with accompaniment
crackling grill & cackling sisters & careening kids
my mother laughing laughing at old jokes
on land stolen to be an israeli army camp
in the outskirts of beit sahour
& we can still see the watchtower looming over area c
but tonight "c" is for "cover me"
which i do when baba gets cold at عش غراب
& hamdillah now he's in the next room sleeping
because outside our love i cannot rest

refrain

after 10 pm the house quiets down. my father lays in his bed, sometimes twitching, sometimes sleeping, sometimes both. the anti-bed sore air mattress huffs & puffs beneath him. its symphony is punctuated by the sound of my mother's phone. she is playing candy crush, or wordscapes, or online poker on one of her three devices. this enables her to have constant access to one game or another, one charged device always at hand. i would like to see her play them all at the same time, some kind of distraction DJ, but instead she swaps between the three, murmuring about the stupidity of each. sometimes i hear stray dogs barking. if i stay up long enough, i hear the أذان. in the morning i hear the bells of the roman orthodox church.

by 10 am the house is loud. my uncle, my father's younger brother (73 years young), comes every morning bearing a fresh bag of pitas. he works at the bakery across the street. his voice is always belligerent. GOOD MORNING HOW ARE YOU قرد يناولك لأخوه. my father never responds to him. my uncle takes it personally, but it has been so many mornings of this personal injury that he shrugs it off & leaves the room. i try to imagine how it feels when someone you love cannot or will not see you, but i don't need to imagine.

amo asks جاية عندنا تنامي ؟ i am in my room feigning sleep like i am 16 instead of 36. or, as my father used to joke, 16 with 20 years experience. my uncle smokes on the veranda with my mother before leaving. if it is a monday, wednesday, or friday two young men come to our home before noon. the first bathes my father, shaves his face, & dresses him. when he leaves, the second man comes & stretches my father's body. hussam turns his head, pulls on his legs, pushes against his shoulders. he walks my father, who teeters on the balls of his feet like a gazelle, between the two living rooms in my parent's home. back & forth. despite all his stretching, my father's shoulders ride high on his neck. he cannot relax.

his foreign body is made stranger by hussam's constant rearranging. his dominion over his limbs ever receding. often during PT my mother plays old arabic music on one of her devices. sometimes hussam sings along, a line or two. during these exchanges my father is silent, focused on the contortions his body achieves at someone else's will. if there is no music playing, we hear the hum of the living. the refrigerator cools, the hot water boils, the birds chirp, the cars honk. a stray shout from the street, an unusually timed phone call.

when hussam leaves my father lays in his bed, recovering. by this time the house is concerned with lunch & the kitchen starts talking. dishes clang in the sink. the gas stove ticks as it ignites. maybe i fry eggs. maybe the pressure cooker steams. my father coughs, as if to clear his throat but words never come. maybe his tremors are starting. we ask: are you hungry? are you thirsty? do you need to use the bathroom? do you want to lay down? do you want to sit up? we plead: you're ok. it's ok. everything is fine. you are fine. it's ok. we flex his hands from their vise grip on the sheets, on his مسبحة, on one another: relax إرتاح! relax. there is nothing to worry about.

there is always music in the afternoon. my father lived in egypt in the late 60s. he was there for college. recently i discovered a cache of photos of him there. posing with the pyramids, mean mugging the camera with his friends. smiling, laughing, studious. my father loves egyptian cinema classics. he would skip class & watch them. he remembers the songs of his 20s. oum kulthum, fairuz, asmahan, farid el atrache, abdel halim. we play them over & over. sometimes his voice is a broken record. he repeats a sound AH AH AH because he loves singing, or because we love for him to sing. it's hard to tell anymore. sometimes one particular song will register on his tongue & he can form his AHs into words. he sings إنت عمري. he sings أعطني الناي. he sings سوّاح. when these do not work, we sing folk songs instead. my aunt, like my uncle, does this at volume. he starts at her voice in his ear, his fingers flickering. she loves him so much. she wants to reach him & this is the only way she knows how.

on tuesday afternoon i play سيدي منصور by saber al raba'ee. it's a newer song, but we danced to it at my cousin's wedding. even though it's

14

not really about fathers, all the babas sprinkled throughout make it seem like it could be. i sing it to him & dance while he sits in his recliner. he reaches up to me, like he wants to dance. we stand together & sway for a while. he's smiling. i'm smiling. he is having a pretty good day. he is eating & singing & sitting. he is able to walk with only one person supporting him. he is having a pretty good day. later that night, after everyone is sleeping, i sob into my pillow. i download wordscapes on my phone & play it on silent until the call to prayer comes around 5 am.

the good days are followed by inversely bad ones. his attention & physical capacity are finite & take a few days to renew. wednesday & thursday are a nightmare. he is shaking & sweating & agitated all day. he is so tired he is falling asleep in his recliner. he can't keep his eyes open to do anything. he doesn't want to eat & every bite is a herculean effort. he forgets to chew. he forgets to swallow. he coughs & chokes & his eyes water. i can never tell if my father is crying anymore. he doesn't recognize anyone. he is not singing. he is not even moaning. he is just shaking & sweating, his fingers clamped & his eyes unfocused. my sister comes over while everyone is at my uncle's & calms him down with songs & whispers. he eats a real meal. he smiles. when everyone returns from my uncle's house it gets loud again & his smile & laughter hover at the edge of mania. when they leave he crashes. he is so soaked in anxiety we change his entire outfit.

on friday, shower & stretch. physically, he's having a good day. mentally, he is somewhere else. very little hooks into his consciousness, just some of our tried & true jokes. one about how he greeted customers at our convenience store in burton. another about where he's hidden the family money, which of course doesn't exist. but it's a good dream. he keeps all his secrets & the day passes without once hearing his voice.

my father was always singing

[folk songs & church songs
& nursery songs
his lilting voice alive with lyric]

hey you!   miss sue!
miss sue from ala-baa-ma
                              let's make a moo-vie

chicka boom chicka boom
boom boom boom

hey mejdu!

[baba called my name]

hey mejdu!

[i loved this game]

hey mejdu!   you're wanted on the pho-one
if it ain't my daddy   tell 'em i'm not home

[in the car he clapped time
against the steering wheel]

hey mejdu!

[what you gonna do]

hey mejdu!

[it's coming for you]

mama's got the measles
daddy's got the flu
god's not lying
                              & neither are you

sitting at the table   peeling my potatoes
watching the clock go tick   tock

[how do you measure time when your father is dying]

tick   tock

[how can your father be dying]

sha wallah wallah

[walla i didn't know miss sue was arab too]

[walla i would do anything to turn back the clock]

tick   tock

[allah can you freeze time]

tick   tock

[yalla]

freeze

first death

on the third day men come to the house wearing suits & sobriety/ sit under the grape vines & seedo's lemon tree/ مسابح their / صلي smoke rothmans (his preferred brand)/ drink فنجان ورا فنجان / the women are indoors & on the veranda/ wear all black/ cry/ make another pot

/ i wear baba's black jeans & a black tee/ we haven't turned on the radio or television since/ i start to put mousse in my hair & baba stops me/ we don't adorn our grief/ on the seventh day we walk/ the church is full/ the casket is closed/

day forty/ baba has gone back to the US/ we are still in school/ it is almost christmas/ we skip the tree & the lights & the presents/ mama gives my brother a stocking away from prying eyes/ he is so little/ the house seedo built holds us/ its dusty marble is cold/ amo fouad had whisky on ice right until the end

/ october/ six months become one year/ they play a dirge at church & mama can't stop crying/ that song/ that song/ she shelves her black wardrobe/ baba comes home/ my sister gets married/ there are men on the lawn & women in the living room/ we learned how to live like this /

what will

in amreeka only grief grows/ manifests/ gathers like weeds/
cracks into everything

at the convenience store you were suffocating/ the low ceilings
dropping/ you would have died there/ you could still// sometimes
the floor surges up around you// you let it

your father turned the soil/ turned the day// your baba/ a
farmer// you are not like him/ but you look like him/ thin hair
thick nose/ wide sturdy feet/ pale skin/ his sun spots on your
hands

you till the soil of yourself/ you water it with your grief/ you
cannot hold him here// he is passing like the seasons/only barren
land left

where does grief live

welling at the hips   wrapping around your gut

inside your skin   on its surface

pouring out

an umbrella after the rainstorm   you without an umbrella

between fingers the skin chalky   your worries a rosary

the slip of each prayer   thumb to forefinger

your fingers against your forehead   against your heart

each shoulder in turn   a cross on your lips

nestled in your throat   a ball rolling back from your mouth

gathering snow   growing   hitches in your chest

melts in the acid of your stomach

you shiver to release it

purgatory

where will my father go when he dies//my father is dying// i
cannot believe it to be true until it is not anymore/ then it will be
too late to believe anything/ my mother shuttles him from doctor
to doctor from bed to bathroom & back/

who is this man who does not look like my father/ i soften when
i see him/ call him habibi as i never did when he was well/ he was
always baba/ strong & fast /the distance between his good hours
& his bad days/ the good shorter & shorter each time//

dementia is an immigrant's nightmare/ even his brain became
foreign// my mother counts pills/ waits for him to swallow/
checks under his tongue/ he fears sleep/ he fears everything/ on
the phone he tells me نفسي ارتاح // we cannot bear his respite/ we
will do anything to hold him here/

my mother calls to him/ keeps him apace in our world when he
travels elsewhere/ she feeds him though his appetite is waned/
the skin slack in his legs & waist/ against old photos he is barely
recognizable// where will my father go when he dies

dementia is a trial run with dying/ a short disappearance/ when
he comes back/ he could be anyone/ he could be your father/
bright with laughter/ calling you by name/ he could be a stranger/
lost & disoriented from travel// i cannot follow him there// we
hold our breath & pray he returns

ekphrastic

baba sits between his remaining siblings/ a bench outside
church/ gathered in amman for a wedding/ his tie loose around
his neck/ his clothes loose around his body/ after muscle loss
but before immobility/ short legs kicked out before him/ like a
kid playing hooky/ skipping chemistry class instead of leading
it// baba used to teach// picture him with the other faculty/ baba
studious/ dark hair falling over forehead/ handsome face/ the
object of 100 crushes/

at the wedding he looks away/ he is someplace else/ maybe
he is thinking about his wife/ sitting tightly next to him/ how
they met/ how he tutored her in math/ how they fell in love/
maybe he is a boy/ playing in the field with brothers/ plotting
with his sister/ متفقين على ظلال / causing chaos/ endearing it to
him/ a dimple on his cheek/ deep enough to fall into// he smiles
often/ he is from an era where masculinity is measured/ in stoic
emotion// baba/ a different kind of man// حنون/

now his mouth has two postures/ his lips compressed together/
anxious control/ or its absence/ a muscle relaxed/ a corner fixed
& a corner dropped/ a smirk without intention/ without agent/
neither of these new smiles are baba// his doctors say mini
strokes/ ignited his dementia/ accelerated it// you cannot slow
it/ cannot slow erasure// water where it ought not be/ an angle
unforgiving/ an erosion

in a few years/ every version of my father will die/ you will look
for signs/ isolate them to the bone/ the muscle above it// still you
will not see// you will not see it coming

what makes the oil boil

in arabish the letter b is a joke/ everywhere we blace it/ tongue
freshly foreign/ fresh off the boat// b as in berfect/ b as in
balestine/ b as in balad/ b as in bernard

before his death baba/ makes you bromise/ you will become his
boet/ with everyday unfulfilled/ like a bresto mounting bressure/
boiling bursting bruising// your grief comes like this/
erubting seebing sbilling

b as in *broud of you, baba*/ b as in burial/ b as in bereaved// what
will i become/ when my father dies// a ghost/ a grief/ a lost// a
sorrow/ a crow/ a sparrow

b as in balash/ b as in bas khalas bikaffi/ b as in breathe/ b as in
blease

prayer for my father's dementia

here is my mouth like a womb gushing its fruit/ birthed but not
borne/ no forsaken daughters/ no patience ripped from the very
bone// god grant him this easy bearing/ a coaxing/

here are my hands like a stake around the vine/ gentle hold/
a fruit free of bruising// should the wind sway us/ no matter/
where the fruit falls it seeds next season/

here is my chest like the earth/ rich dark humus/ petrichor
soothes tight lungs// would the wind plant him here/ grounded
for generations/

here are my feet like platforms/ raised up over rugged waters/ &
you do not belong here// still floating after an exile almost killed
us/

here is my blood like tides on the ocean/ pink chasing the
horizon/ a sun setting & rising/ i give myself back to salt// we
color heaven until it is a riot of light/

notes

my father Bernard Farid Shomali was diagnosed with Lewy body dementia in 2014. it progressed rapidly and disappeared him in a few short years. my father was a Palestinian immigrant to the US. he trained as an agricultural engineer but operated a convenience store in Michigan. he returned to Palestine shortly after his diagnosis, which came two years after his retirement. in 2022, he died and was laid to rest, as he wished, in Palestine. my father taught me Arabic and kept it alive for me in diaspora. he instilled in me a love of language and song. he is also responsible for my love of our homeland and my vexed relationship to faith. my work would not be possible without him. i am endlessly thankful for him.

the publication acceptance for this chapbook arrived on the one-year anniversary of my father's death. thank you to Finishing Line Press for giving the chapbook a home and to Marwa Helal for shepherding it into its current form. my sincere gratitude to Aude Abou Nasr for designing the cover. many thanks to my poetry comrades who've read and offered comments on various poems in the collection. i am grateful to Palestinian and Arab writers whose voices made space for mine.

mejdulene bernard shomali is a queer Palestinian poet and associate professor in women's, gender, and sexuality studies at Williams College. she is the author of *Between Banat: Queer Arab Critique and Transnational Arab Archives* (Duke University Press 2023).

www.ingramcontent.com/pod-product-compliance
Lightning Source LLC
Chambersburg PA
CBHW022101080426
42734CB00009B/1439